ABANDONED INDIANA

JAY FARRELL

AMERICA
THROUGH TIME®
ADDING COLOR TO AMERICAN HISTORY

America Through Time is an imprint of Fonthill Media LLC
www.through-time.com
office@through-time.com

Published by Arcadia Publishing by arrangement with Fonthill Media LLC
For all general information, please contact Arcadia Publishing:
Telephone: 843-853-2070
Fax: 843-853-0044
E-mail: sales@arcadiapublishing.com
For customer service and orders:
Toll-Free 1-888-313-2665

www.arcadiapublishing.com

First published 2020

ISBN 978-1-63499-199-5

Typeset in Trade Gothic 10pt on 15pt
Printed and bound in England

CONTENTS

ABOUT THE AUTHOR

Jay Farrell is a Nashville, Tennessee, based photographer who loves photographing abandoned structures. He has a passion for utilizing his camera to share the unique, distressed beauty of abandoned homes and structures that most of the world has forgotten. Sharing his adventures with the public through authorship and blogging inspires him as much as the adventures themselves.

INTRODUCTION

The "life after people" feel to abandoned buildings—complete with rotted and caving floors, forgotten contents of yesteryear, and the overall entropy and distress—are what fuels my inspiration. There's a freedom (and a danger) of hitting the open road and exploring the backroad to seek these abandoned treasures. These structures tell a story. My goal while photographing these structures is to tell those stories and be their voice after they've been forgotten, sometimes for generations.

There is a process to my work. I don't force my way in or vandalize and I don't take or disturb anything. This shows a level of respect and reduces liability. These places are sometimes a hideout for squatters or vandals, which adds potential danger to the situation. It's extremely rare for me to be confronted by an heir or property owner, but it can happen. The structures are dangerous, with roofs caving in, broken glass, nails, needles, wildlife, loose boards, and weak floors. You must know what is under your feet—another reason I prefer to go with a trusted colleague if that option is available. It's eerie; there are lots of noises, creaks, and constant echoes.

This book features the work from my travels and adventures in Indiana, exploring the narrow farm backroads and industrial streets that only the locals travel. I will take you with me on the journey through some of the most dilapidated structures that most people only imagine. You will enjoy an exciting mix of forlorn farmhouses, rusted remains of ruined factories, and a small town gas station.

It's not for the faint of heart, but the walls always tell stories and I enjoy the adventures. In this book, I will make my audience part of the adventure. I take you up close and personal to these tumbling structures, far deeper than the roadside view. Through my lens, you will experience the true, authentic feel of the Hoosier State. I hope you enjoy it!

Take only pictures, leave only footprints. [*Illustration by Kelly J. King*]

1

MECHANIC NOT ON DUTY

My friend Chris moved from Nashville to Southeast Indiana several years ago, which has made get-togethers rare, but we always pick up where we left off. When he lived local to me, we'd go on canoe trips, he'd pass along his chef skills, and we'd grill out together. Our conversations always went deeper and far more analytical than normal. Assuming any of us know, or care to know, what normal is. But I don't think a fly on the wall would ever be bored by our conversations.

I took a long weekend in September, which officially meant autumn weather in Indiana, to visit Chris. We both needed a break and needed inspiration, so what better way to find it than to do an abandoned building excursion with a long-time friend and photography mentor? I drove to Lawrenceburg to visit him, and there was beer and a bonfire waiting for me the night I arrived. The next morning, we had breakfast at an old-time diner and set out on our mission.

Our first stop was an abandoned gas station/car repair shop that has surely been abandoned for at least a decade. Its state of disrepair and distress due to Mother Nature taking over, vandalism, and building materials of yesteryear all kept its story alive. I remember it was right on the Ohio state line. I walked to the sign, jumped back and forth, and put one leg on each side, before I got serious about my business.

They forgot to put the "closed" sign up, but I think most people would figure it out.

The office/store portion of the building with peeling paint and busted glass.

The lone light bulb that hasn't given up, under a roof that clearly is giving up.

I love the steel beam and fallen boards; industrial construction is perhaps my favorite.

The defunct electrical box.

This is an old air-powered grease gun, mainly for lubricating the chassis during routine oil changes.

Yup, Satanists have made it to Indiana, too, and I found them on my first stop. Lucky me!

Sometimes color brings out the character of a photograph and displays texture/patina just as well as black and white, if not better in this case.

Left: Steel industrial doors are something you don't see much anymore.

Below: You haven't lived until you have to ask the attendant for the restroom key and sit on a toilet like this one in 10-degree weather.

This close-up of reinforced industrial glass shares a unique texture with the rusted steel window frame. I may make a print of this to display in my house.

I really enjoyed this stop. I'm not one to take any longer than needed, but Chris reminded me that we had exhausted our resources and there was more to see. It's amazing how the comfort level changes when discretion isn't as much of a concern, at any given abandoned property. Normally I have an uncanny sense of that on my own.

2

BABY BLUE

After exploring several desolate, remote Midwest backroads, we spotted this old Victorian-style farmhouse. Because of its happy, cheerful color, there wasn't any way to make the exterior look extremely sinister and creepy, despite its level of distress. This meant that I needed to get inside to bring out the sinister feel of this charming, welcoming old house.

The other rooms were completely bare, and kitchen appliances and cabinets were ripped out. This isn't the first time I've seen special houses like this with uncompleted projects. It's one thing to have an idea, and another thing to have the funds and skills to complete the project. Mold had set in and structural damage had been progressing over the years. I knew soon the options would be demolition or someone finishing the project before it completely fell apart.

Approximately one year after our excursion that day, Chris told me that someone bought that old farmhouse and had been fixing it up nicely. I was glad to hear that, but was even gladder to have captured it in its previous distressed state. I'm no historian, but in a sense, I document history. Abandoned houses and buildings are burned down, demolished, fall down on their own, or in rare cases, are restored—especially if the house has remarkable features, like this house did.

Above: Charming and welcome old farmhouse on the outside. I was eager to see what awaited us inside.

Right: Yes! This was some of the sinister mood I was hoping to capture. This was a brilliant staircase.

Above: I thought it was interesting that the bathroom had wooden bead board walls. Maybe humidity from showers weren't a concern when the house was built. They were holding up well, along with this funky colored sink.

Left: The upstairs hallway was a bit haunting, particularly with roof and structural issues. Layers of paint, plaster, and wallpaper added to the character.

3

THE SETTLERS

During the late 1700s, in the Revolutionary War era, settlers arrived in the area, and Lawrenceburg was soon officially founded. Those settlers built this stone house that still stands in the middle of a very large field, built from stone from the field and creek. There is also a cemetery across the road with all the names of the settlers. Despite dealing with hostility from local Indians, which is certainly understandable, they made their home there. Followed by many generations since.

This house was remarkable, and is structurally still standing, though all that remains is the shell. That should be a true testament to quality workmanship. This was a rich experience knowing the age and history, and how rare of a find this is. A paranormal investigator would have a field day here. If there were spirits that remained anywhere, this would be the place. I experienced a handcrafted, custom built home that was over 200 years old, with many textures, colors, and resourceful materials. This makes me wonder what they started with, and when different amenities such as electricity were added. The shell of the house and the plaster are probably all original.

On our final leg of the journey, there was nothing in the way of abandoned houses. But it was fun to see very remote gravel roads with nothing around except complete desolation. If someone wanted to live off the grid, deep in those Indiana backroads would be as good a place as any. It was literally a gravel path cut through the woods and hills. Chris said he remembered seeing these really creepy dolls hanging from trees, which I would have photographed if we were able to find them. I kept on envisioning a clown on the side of the road operating a popsicle stand. In places like this, the few residents there are don't exactly welcome outsiders. It's the nature of this game, I suppose. I don't go to these places to see people either, so we're even.

This was possibly the oldest abandoned house I've encountered.

This reminds me of a very old Irish pub I visited in Dublin.

Above left: A hand-built, very narrow staircase.

Above right: I love the color of the paint on the plaster and texture of the old weathered door.

Below: Beautiful destruction, but it still stands tall.

Above: Overgrowth penetrates the window frame, as the textured wall gets the fall-off light.

Left: An abstract close-up detail of the doorway, complimented by randomly growing brush.

I'm sure this came later, but this is still very old electrical work.

A nice side view of the house with less tree shade and slightly less vegetation taking over.

4

THE TIME CAPSULE

After an eighteen-month hiatus from my last exploration in Indiana, I made an impromptu journey to Southwest Indiana, mainly to get a feel for the lay of the land. I was not sure what I would find, or if I would find anything abandoned that I was looking for on this trip. This day was about scratching an itch, satisfying my curiosity, and exploratory purposes. It was early April, and one of the first weeks I could comfortably drive with the windows down, feeling the freedom of the road with the wind blowing through my hair. The nice contrast between flat open land with only fields and forests, rolling green hills, and quaint small towns created an enjoyable experience for me.

The adventure continued, navigating through the rural Indiana backroads that were randomly selected by instinct. Suddenly, on a fairly rough, curvy two-lane blacktop, was a very old farmhouse sitting atop a hill which caught my attention immediately. There was one small problem. There was no driveway, or place to park my car, because of a non-existent road shoulder and steep hills surrounding the road. Next door, there was a lady on a tractor cutting the grass for the first time of the season on their farm. No matter what I did, there was nothing obstructing her vision of me at this abandoned farmhouse next door, and the smart thing to do was to introduce myself. This is an extreme rarity for me, especially when there are "beware of dog" and "no trespassing" signs.

Thankfully, the lady was receptive and somewhat intrigued by my reason for being there, then told me the house had been abandoned long before they settled there. She then advised me to park across the road in the pull-off going to their barn, which solved the main problem. The next thing she told me was that she explored the old house once and found many old belongings that creeped her out, then left immediately. At that point I was salivating, and thanked her for her time. The dog was friendly, too—double victory.

The first glance as I trekked up the hill. My first thought was that I have not seen lightning rods in ages.

The front porch has some structural issues overhead, but in all fairness, they didn't expect company that day.

From the back angle, Denise, the lady next door, spotted me from across the field and was probably wondering if I was crazy enough to go inside. Never bet against me. Yes, I am.

You would not normally see me photographing flowers, or anything pretty, as the world sees it. However, I couldn't help but notice the juxtaposition of the perennial daffodils that someone once lovingly planted along the perimeter of the long-forgotten home.

Apparently someone needed the doorknob more than this house did.

Chicken Little may be exaggerating about the sky falling, but this roof and porch certainly are.

Handywork of a chicken house or doghouse—I'm not sure which.

This barn is next to the old farmhouse. Just seconds before I took this photograph, a large buzzard flew out of the barn window, making a racket. He looked at me and let me know that I have something he wants, if I were to fall over and not get back up. Always comforting.

Gently touched by the afternoon sun.

You're always welcome to stay here. There's a bed waiting for you. Thanks, but no thanks.

Above: These very old work boots and other belongings left behind had my undivided attention. My undivided attention is not easy to get, in most cases.

Below left: This vintage 1960s refrigerator would be a picker's dream, but maybe not after having to empty forty-plus-year-old contents. Soon, you will know how I know this.

Below right: A closer look at the metal ice trays, plastic egg cartons, and 1970s ketchup and salad dressing jars/ bottles.

It was eerie seeing all the old clothes hanging up in random places in the house. There was a lot of unfinished business there.

The calendar stopped at December 1976. This could be a very accurate timeline of when the house was abruptly abandoned. There were many newspapers strewn about from that era as well.

Is it normal for an old pharmaceutical bottle and a C or D cell battery to sit in the windowsill? Maybe not, but these people were okay with it.

The kitchen was oozing with old items from the cupboard and whatever else you could think of.

Right: I can picture a hot, dusty, and humid summer day with windows open, and the flies wouldn't leave them alone. They probably got their money's worth from that old fly swatter.

Below: Grandma and grandpa's living room chair still sits in the same spot. I wonder if they ever had a television.

Old couches in surprisingly intact condition, yes.

This isn't a likely vagrant location, but the mattress looks newer than anything in the house, so it's possible there has been some activity since the former occupants vanished.

Layers of wallpaper and plaster.

There are a lot of beds in the house, in other rooms besides the bedrooms. This makes me wonder if the former residents were elderly shut-ins.

Left: The kitchen cupboard with nothing but pure retro ingredients. That box of Ivory Snow has to be from the 1970s as well!

Below: Shouldn't cans of oil be in the barn? Mystery here.

Above left: This was nearly a subject of controversy. I thought nothing of it while there, but after further review, several of us thought this resembled a Klansman robe. After further research, we think it's a hooded women's' duster jacket. Phew!

Above right: To go upstairs or not to go upstairs. You know I went.

Below left: The upstairs was treated more as attic space than living space.

Below right: Yet more garments tattered by time.

Make yourself comfortable, you may have to share your space with the vultures and raccoons.

There must be a dozen mattresses in this house, including the gutted ones.

Right: There's not a clean inch of floor space in the upstairs hallway, which made my risk of going upstairs worthwhile.

Below: Possibly a 100-year-old door—complete with texture, distress, and patina—still standing.

5

HELL ON THE HILL

I was buzzing with excitement after leaving the last farmhouse, as history was made in many respects. I continued to navigate different combinations of backroads, even some unpaved roads with only numbers, not names. My direction was not clear, but I was nearing the point in the journey that I needed to not go further away from home, even if it meant traveling different roads to go the proper direction. A faded road sign said "Perry County" as I was leaving Spencer County. There were a couple of different rural roads that looked promising, so I explored them before changing direction towards Western Kentucky. On the final country road I explored, I saw a very old Victorian-era house with dilapidate wood siding, and all kinds of structural problems visible from the road.

Many people would take one look at this old abandoned house and go the other way because of how creepy or haunted it looks. The former driveway was eroded and filled in by weeds, on a slightly muddy hillside. Fortunately, I was able to get my car off the road far enough and walk up to the old house, hoping the area was as desolate as it looked. That's one nice thing about exploring the abandoned in the countryside. The downside is that you're on your own if something happens. It seems like a fair tradeoff.

The wind and the crunching sound under my feet as I walk across the rough brushy terrain were the only sounds, until I entered the house.

It's usually at a house like this in the middle of a huge field, where aliens choose to land.

The front porch was completely rotted, and now I see the back porch is as well. At that time, I wasn't sure there was another way in, but I am persistent.

Maybe on this side of the porch; hope isn't lost yet.

Right: This door might open, but it probably falls before it shuts.

Below: The fact that this house still stands is largely due to its quality construction back in the good old days.

I didn't expect to find an antique manual washing machine just laying outside, but sometimes you never know.

The jackpot keeps getting better. This early 1970s Ford Mustang sits in the back yard with no wheels, seemingly forgotten about.

It was time to focus on getting inside, I finally found a way. All I needed to do was climb over that large heater and hope I didn't fall through the sunken floor.

There was no shortage of decrepit appliances and living room furniture in the kitchen. I'm not sure how the floors held all that weight, so I felt confident that I wouldn't make a huge difference.

At this point, I was so glad I randomly traveled this road.

I climbed over that couch to get into the living room, and continued to walk gingerly.

That was as far as I could walk on that side without falling through, so I went back in the living room.

A deep freezer in the living room? Whatever you like is fine with me. It probably served more as a barricade for the door. Spoiler alert: This urban explorer outsmarted the system.

I'd gladly stay for a game of Life, but there was no opponent. There hasn't been one in a long time, I'm guessing.

The final parting gift from this humble abode, a late 70s/early 80s television.

6

WORSE FOR WEAR

Occasionally, when I'm ready to wrap up the adventure for the day and return home, I must investigate just one more unexpected abandoned sighting that I wasn't even looking for. While traveling the highway that would have brought me across the Ohio River, back into Kentucky, I saw a magnificent dilapidated house on a service road. I thought to myself, "Why not? I'm here." I exited the highway and found the service road, using a farm equipment dealer next door to the house as a reference.

The farm equipment sales facility was closed for the day, and there wasn't a soul around, so the vicinity was mine to explore. The old house was in very poor structural condition. The fact that it was still standing defied the laws of physics, and was a testament to how well it was built. When I concluded this part of my excursion, I crossed the mighty Ohio River, and drove off into the sunset. This impromptu, exploratory journey was the best thing I could have done that day, and I already looked forward to my next trek to Indiana.

Above: This ramshackle old house was in worse structural condition up close than what I saw from the road, to no one's surprise.

Left: It's a good thing I got here when I did, as I don't see how this place will stand much longer. I was very glad I made the stop.

I suppose it's safe to say that there was no inside to this house any longer.

I am not sure how many more strong winds this crumbling house can withstand.

Above: This was all that was left of the inside. I tried climbing in through the window. As soon as I did, I felt my foot sink into the floor, which was no real surprise. I was happy to take my photograph from where I sat.

Left: Around back, the dynamic doesn't change much.

I contacted the farm equipment sales dealer to gather more information. The lady said they bought the land twenty years ago, and the house was long since abandoned then. The back-porch appliances were just a bonus.

It took me a moment to figure out what this was—a power supply for an electrified cattle fence.

7

THE STARVING ARTIST

Nashville had moderate rain the morning my friend, Jerry Winnett, and I left for Indiana to explore, with partly cloudy conditions awaiting us there. Two different people I knew suggested exploring Brown County, with Nashville as the county seat. It was ironic, but we traveled from Nashville to Nashville. Nashville, Indiana, was approximately 90 miles north of Louisville, after crossing the Ohio River.

On the main stretch towards Nashville, there were many newer retail businesses. Nashville was an adorable, quaint tourist area with many small shops, restaurants, art galleries, and other attractions that drew thousands of people on that seasonable April afternoon. Jerry and I were thinking that whoever sent us there must not have been there in recent years, as we had the feeling the area went through gentrification. We were already there, so we navigated many back roads as soon as we could find them. Our findings were closer to what we were looking for, but there were minimal abandoned properties. There were also quite a few new construction houses built on land, which may have been overspill from Indianapolis, an hour north of Brown County.

It was time to decide that we enjoyed exploring a new place, but cut our losses and go back the direction we came to somewhere different. Cell service was unreliable as far out in the weeds we were traveling, so we relied on true north as much as possible. While attempting to navigate back towards the interstate, and move onto a new area, this picturesque faded yellow farmhouse appeared out of nowhere. The house was long past the point of inhabitation, but the land surrounding the old forlorn farmhouse was well kept. The neighboring cattle were watching, and I had that feeling that other eyes may have been upon us, but it was time to get the scoop on this place.

Full of character and perched on the hilltop.

The back porch, complete with 1980s bug zapper.

Left: Side porch entrance, with one problem: The floor was rotted badly.

Below: The siding and gutters telling a tale of distress.

Circa early 1900s house, equipped with original wavy glass windows still in place.

Wasps nests took over the once-stocked bird feeder.

Left: This got us in the back porch, but the entrance door into the house was locked.

Below: Goodbye old paint. I'm sure it's dried up by now, and probably has been for decades.

Above: I love the look of this old shop basin, used to clean up before coming in for dinner.

Right: The old mercury thermometer still worked, but the bird's nest has been vacated.

Left: Bob Ross inspired, no doubt.

Below: The kitchen cabinets were bare. As was the rest of the house.

I'm not sure about carpet in the bathroom, or their attempt at color coordinating their fixtures, but it's their house.

This one painting was all that remained on the walls.

Left: A creepy staircase entrance. Nothing was upstairs either.

Below: The sun shines on the slowly germinating trees and reflects on the weathered wood siding.

8

CLEARANCE PAINT

When Jerry and I were approximately 40 miles north of Louisville, Kentucky, where we decided to explore next, we made the necessary fuel stop. We were surrounded by flat, desolate open land, and decided to explore some backroads in that area first. The geography was different from Brown County, and more closely resembled the Southwest Indiana region I explored previously.

The elements were in place. Warm air, overcast skies, growing green grass, straight backroads and a huge horizon line. We were in close proximity of the Jackson/Jennings County line, and spotted an old white house surrounded by some brush. There was no question this house had been abandoned for ages. Behind it was a gutted trailer house, and there were two utility sheds on the side of the house. This stop turned out to be fruitful, and was a good luck charm going into Louisville.

A rather odd-looking house, but certainly interesting and intriguing. The prickly bushes made the trek to the front porch a bit uncomfortable, but that goes with territory.

It's always a bit weird to think of how someone lovingly made this bird house and hung curtains. Now all of it sits waiting to deteriorate.

Scavengers have ransacked the heat and air conditioning unit, wiring, and utility lines containing metals. Nothing unusual.

Utility barn number one, currently housing trash and debris.

The inside view, possibly made more catastrophic by squatters or an heir. Much like the side and back yards.

The inside of the second utility barn, apparently used as a canning kitchen. The entrance door was extra thick, reminiscent of a lighter wooden bank vault door. They meant business.

There are always many sample color cards in paint stores, even when this house was painted inside. To think that someone chose this color is unfathomable. The mold developed over time, of course.

I suppose it would be too much to ask to make me a sandwich?

A fallen door, which was far more solid to walk on than the concave floors.

The conversation pit could use some tidying, but it's cozy.

I wouldn't usually walk in someone else's house and laugh at their terrible decorating skills, but I was left with no choice here. Nobody here would know anyway.

About that trip grandpa promised he'd make some day—sadly, it never happened.

I don't remember whose turn it was to do dishes, but they forgot to put them away.

Above: Perhaps this was a separate kitchen before the air conditioning days. I found newspapers from 1990 on the floor. This could be a very accurate timeline clue.

Right: The back breezeway, complete with sunken floor and old water heater.

The yard work of an heir or squatters, who knows which.

Office and desk with scenic view.

Someone's been sleeping in my bed.

I loved the abstract pattern of the vines growing on the bead board porch ceiling.

9

PYROMANIA AT THE PIANO FACTORY

I felt it was only appropriate to provide a variety of content, and compliment the forgotten rural Indiana farmhouses with its forgotten factories. My first thought was Gary, Indiana, which I still may do. However, a different author in this series did a dedicated book on abandoned Gary, and I wanted to keep my content as original as possible. Upon doing my research on other industrial Indiana cities of yesteryear, I learned that many cities demolished or repurposed the abandoned factories, which is happening almost everywhere to an extent. The detective work continued.

My friend in Indianapolis put me in contact with a relative in Muncie, 50 miles northeast of Indianapolis, who is a local historical enthusiast. I enjoyed chatting it up with Aidan about abandoned properties and history, both learning from each other. He was fascinated with the idea of photographing abandoned locations, which I could teach him a lot about. In turn, he shared his knowledge of the area and history with me. The day finally came¾I took a trip to Muncie, we eagerly met up to go exploring, and I brushed up on my Muncie geography.

By the early 1900s, Muncie was one of the most industry rich cities in the Midwest per capita. The booming blue-collar community had many factories and industries that employed its residents. The railroads, Chevrolet, Ball Company, Borg Warner, Indiana Steel and Wire, Broderick Boiler Company, and more, were major local employers. They are now distant echoes of Muncie's industrial heyday. Manufacturing, steel, fabrication, glass manufacturing, even automotive, put Muncie on the map. Over the years, manufacturing has changed, and companies and factories shut down or moved out of Muncie, whose economy never recovered as a result.

Most of the defunct factories which housed notable local employers have been razed or repurposed, as an attempt to introduce new blood to the struggling, once thriving industrial city. Aidan and I visited the rusted remains of any known remaining local Muncie manufacturing/industrial icons. We started with a burned piano factory, according to my research. More history can be found in the captions.

It's ironic, to say the least, to see a fire hydrant system at the entry point of a burned down factory.

This building (or what remains) was built in 1895, and became the Bell Brothers Piano Company, known for manufacturing high-end pianos. After financial troubles that led to the company's demise, the building was taken over by Warner Machine. In more recent years, the building was used for a pallet and skid manufacturing plant.

Left: You know that fire was fully involved when a steel industrial door is mangled from the intense heat. The fire was caused by arson in 2014. Several years before that, the building was taken out of service due to structural problems, and was used for storage. Flammable and combustible materials left on site made the fire a chore to extinguish.

Below: A freight elevator sits on what used to be the building slab, no longer surrounded by walls.

Above: I suppose the no smoking sign is completely moot at this point.

Right: It's human nature to at least try to operate the controls even though you know they aren't going to work. Of course I did.

Above: The boiler room still stood, and seemed relatively unaffected by the fire.

Left: This tower stood strong still.

The other side that was clearly adjoined with the rest of the building at one time.

Those four stories looked gigantic from where I stood looking up.

The basement level of the room next to the tower has been taken over by copious amounts of rubble and ponding water.

Inside the boiler room—always one of my favorite areas of any industrial location.

I wonder if workers ever came up with a name for this beast of a boiler. Maybe Bertha. Or something less predictable?

It may have been many years since factory workers used this workbench, but it was still standing proud.

This rotting old chair probably got its fair share of use for cigarette and lunch breaks, or an employee trying to get away from the boss for a minute.

Color, texture, patina, and amateur graffiti. No missing ingredients.

10

THE BOILER FACTORY

Our next destination was the former Broderick Boiler factory. Our most discreet point of entry required walking through desolate greenway paths, under an old railroad bridge, and hiking up a wooded hill. There was one small problem. The entire perimeter was fenced off, and there was barbed wire atop the fence. I told Aidan that if we were patient, we would find a spot that someone cut out or a spot to go under. Sure enough, we found our meal ticket. The journey in wasn't over just yet, however. There were "Keep Out" signs all over the place, and another fence surrounding the weathered factory. Thankfully, the gate was unlocked.

This is the former home of the Broderick Company, where Broderick boilers were made, since 1905. As railroad service expanded in Muncie to factories like Broderick Company, business was booming, and Broderick was a major employer for Muncie residents. In 1934, Broderick acquired Dean Forging, and continued automotive forgings, until World War II began. During that time, both plants concentrated on manufacturing weapons for war. Incidentally, automobiles were not being manufactured in America during the war era, so that all available steel could be used for weapons.

As we walked the perimeter of this once prospering factory, admiring its features, we were faced with the reality of inside access being impossible. The good news is my lens fit in through a couple of small broken windows. There was more to see on the exterior, as the inside was mostly an empty shell. Having Aidan with me gave me a great local perspective that helped personalize this chapter with information only a local would know. His grandfather worked at the factory in the 1960s and shared some stories with him that I will reveal in the corresponding photo captions. This old factory was long gone, but moved many tons of steel in its day.

The railroad that serviced the Broderick Factory. Along the way, we spotted abandoned railroad markers in the woods.

These huge perches were outside the plant to hold the gas containers that were gravity fed. When the tank was elevated on the perches, the bottom of the containers were tapped. The caps on the ground are what was left of the containers.

Above: The back side of the Broderick factory, after getting through the first fence.

Left: That press was probably very persuasive in its day.

Above: Bar stock steel was delivered by train, stored in the steel shed, and brought in the factory using a trolley system on small tracks.

Right: I have to hand it to the caretakers of this property: They crossed almost every *T* and dotted most every *i* when it comes to keeping people out. They even removed the lower section of the industrial ladders.

Left: Fences and other metal fabrication blocked every point of entry. But by now I was ok with that, as the outside was so fascinating.

Below: These tough old steel girders acted as the rail system for the crane that loaded steel into the trolleys and steel shed.

Above left: Even if I had all of that, I don't think they'd let me in.

Above right: I can hear these chains clanking, with workers yelling and machinery running, all non-stop until quitting time.

Below: This is the steel shed where the trolleys were used. Aidan's grandfather remembers a worker unfortunately losing his leg when the trolley tipped over and crushed it. That sounds excruciating to say the least.

Left: These industrial doors with character and texture always photograph well on their own.

Below: This steel shed roof can get no more primal and industrial.

With part of the "do" list blocked, no wonder they had workplace accidents.

Aidan's grandfather also remembers when the crane got stuck and fell off the rails. That and the poor bloke who lost his leg were just two of the horror stories we know about. Factory safety and efficiency are why many have relocated to a more modern facility in recent years.

Just the perfect amount of rust and grime to make a beautiful work of art.

This rusted old hydraulic press has seen a lot of action in the past. Now it just sits there and looks pretty.

Still looking for my way in, these windows were slightly above eye level.

I believe you mean, "You are on camera." You're welcome.

At least they spelled that one right, but I came too far not to take the chance.

On a sunny day, that fan would cast an interesting shadow on the inside before sundown.

I had to aim the lens through the broken windows, but I told you I'd get in, one way or the other, without breaking anything.

This was the most equipment I was able to see.

Someone's doing something in there. Good luck moving that monstrosity of a machine.

What a wonderful treat this was, to experience this legendary factory. If we waited much longer, we may have been too late.

MORE BY JAY FARRELL

ABANDONED ALABAMA

ISBN: 978-1-63499-114-8

ABANDONED KENTUCKY
VOLUME 1

ISBN: 978-1-63499-056-1

ABANDONED KENTUCKY
VOLUME 2

ISBN: 978-1-63499-169-8

MORE BY JAY FARRELL

ABANDONED TENNESSEE
VOLUME 1
ISBN: 978-1-63499-055-4

ABANDONED TENNESSEE
VOLUME 2
ISBN: 978-1-63499-102-5

ABANDONED NASHVILLE
ISBN: 978-1-63499-113-1

ABANDONED MISSISSIPPI
ISBN 978-1-63499-179-7